Grandfather's Stories From Cambodia

Written by Donna Roland
Illustrations by Ron Oden

ISBN O-941996-O5-O
Copyright © 1984
OPEN MY WORLD PUBLISHING
13OO Lorna St., El Cajon, CA 9202O

There is a little boy and a little girl
who go to school just like you do.
The boy's name is Bona, and the
girl's name is Nary.

They go to school just like you do, they dress just like you do, they play games just like you do, but one thing is not the same:

Bona and Nary's family is from Cambodia.

Bona and Nary live in a city with their mother and father and their little brother, whose name is Sorath.

The times Bona and Nary like the most are when Grandfather tells them stories about Cambodia, their homeland far away.

Grandfather tells them happy
stories about the land and its
people. They are stories Bona and
Nary cannot forget.

He tells them how their people have
lived in Cambodia for many, many
years. Bona, Nary, and their little
brother Sorath could sit for hours
hearing their grandfather's stories.

He tells them how their people have
been ruled by many kings and
rulers from other lands.

Grandfather tells them how the sun and moon show their people what time of the year it is. Bona and Nary learn that the shorter months, the months with less than 30 days in them, are the girls' months.

The longer months, with more days in them, are boys' months. Grandfather's people do not ever get married in boys' months; it's bad luck.

Bona and Nary also learn from
Grandfather that in Cambodia
every year begins in April, and
each year is named after one of
twelve animals.

There is the year of the Rat, the Ox, the Tiger,

the Rabbit, the Snake, the Goat, and the Horse.

There is the year of the Monkey, the Rooster, the Dog, the Pig, and

the year of the Dragon.

Grandfather helps Bona and Nary learn about their people and their ways. He tells them that each of them has a place in the world and that they should look for the truth.

One day when Bona and Nary
were trying to help their little brother
learn the days of the week, they
thought of how Grandfather had
told them about each day...

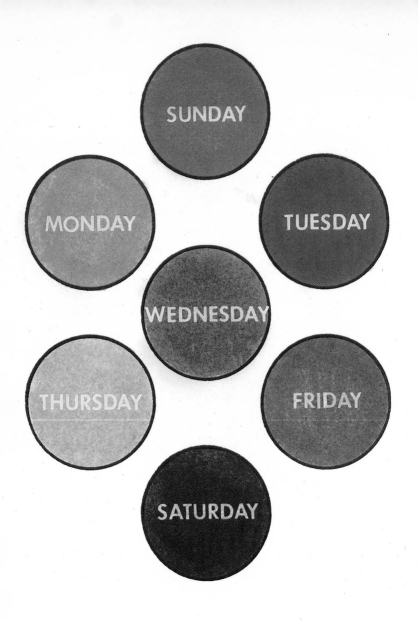

You see, Grandfather's people have a color for each day of the week.

Each day has its own color that is
just for that day. Sunday is the sun's
day and its color is red. Monday is
the moon's day and its color is
orange.

In a few days Sorath had learned all the days of the week. He had also learned something about Cambodia and its people.

Bona and Nary's family lives near
many small houses that are close to
their school. They know that if they
were living in Cambodia, their
home would not look the same.

The houses in Cambodia are made of wood and built on tall legs. The houses are built that way so people can keep their wagons or animals under them. Having the houses so tall also helps keep them dry when the rains come.

It rains a lot in Cambodia. The rain is good for growing rice. Grandfather's people eat rice almost every day. Sometimes they eat rice with fish and sometimes they eat rice with vegetables they have grown in their garden.

Bona and Nary love hearing Grandfather's stories, and Grandfather loves sharing the stories with them. He hopes his family will share his stories because the stories are about their people, their homeland, and searching for the truth.

Bona and Nary have learned that each person in this world has a place and a reason for being here. They have also learned to be truthful with others and to know the truth inside themselves.